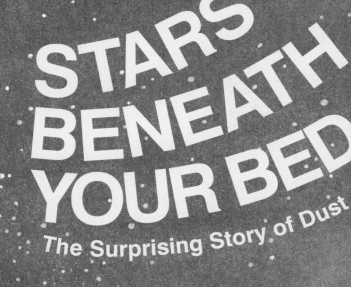

STARS BENEATH YOUR BED

The Surprising Story of Dust

By April Pulley Sayre
Pictures by Ann Jonas

 Greenwillow Books, *An Imprint of HarperCollins Publishers*

At sunrise,
  the sun, low in the sky,
    peeks through dusty air.
      Dust from us and dirt and dinosaurs
        scatters light, painting the sky like fire.

Dust is made everywhere, every day.
A flower drops pollen.
A dog shakes dirt from its fur.
A butterfly flutters,
and scales fall off its wings.

That's dust. Dust is little bits of things.

You and I make dust.
Your bike wheels scatter dust.
Skin, old and dry, flakes from our arms.
Cotton rubs off jeans as we
cartwheel through the grass.
That's dust.
So is dirt from farmers' plows.

**Dust is made in nature
when meerkats dig,
when zebras roll,
when cheetahs chase gazelles across the land.**

Wind picks up dirt and
swirls it in whirlwinds—
dust storms that sweep the savanna.

Dust can be bits of unexpected things—
a crumbling leaf, the eyelash of a seal,
the scales of a snake,
the smoke of burning toast,
ash from an erupting volcano.

Dust can come from the ocean.
An ocean wave breaks.
***Slap!* It splashes salt into the air.**

**Wind carries salt dust up and up—
smell the salty ocean spray!**

Old dust stays around.
   Dust that made King Tut sneeze is still on Earth.
   It might be on your floor.

That dusty film on your computer screen
might have muddied a dinosaur.

Some dust comes from outer space.
The dust beneath your bed might be from Mars.
It could be part of a comet,
or a bit of the moon.
Cosmic dust sifts down from asteroids.

Wind spreads dust,
floating,
swirling,
sprinkling,
bits of you and me
and soil
and stars.

Afternoon light,
    shining through trees,
        shows us dust is there.

All the dust of our day
will scatter light this evening.
Sunset pink. Sunset orange. Sunset red.
The dust of our day
will color the sunset we see.

And tonight will paint
the sunrise of tomorrow.

Dust and Sunsets

Anything smaller than one-sixteenth of a millimeter in diameter is considered dust. Dust is smaller than the period at the end of this sentence. It is smaller than the width of a human hair. Dust can be made up of many things—desert dirt, bark bits, pollen grains, tire rubber, and even bacteria. It can be salt, skin flakes, or little pieces of just about any material you can imagine. Dust may be small, but its impact is large. When the sun is low in the sky, its rays hit dust particles at an angle. This creates the sunset colors we see. The sky colors change as the sun moves, striking the particles at new angles. The same thing occurs at sunrise, because the sun is low in the sky then as well.

The more dust, the more colorful the sunsets and sunrises. When volcanoes erupt or forest fires burn, they send a lot of ash and soot into the air. This ash dust makes sunsets particularly colorful for weeks and even months, until the dust settles. These unusually colorful sunsets can occur hundreds, even thousands of miles from the fires or eruptions. That is because dust travels. Dust from Africa's Sahara Desert floats all the way to Florida. Some say Sahara dust turns Miami rain slightly pink. Sahara dust also lands on Brazil's Amazon rain forest, where it adds nutrients that help the forest grow. Dust from a volcanic eruption, such as that of Mount Saint Helens in Washington State, can circle the entire globe.

Dust not only helps create beautiful sunsets, it helps create rain. Water that evaporates from lakes, streams, oceans, and leaf surfaces rises up into the sky as water vapor. It condenses—becomes liquid again—by attaching to dust particles. Each raindrop needs a piece of dust to form.

Every day, all over the world, dust mixes as air circulates. Because of this mixing, it's likely the dust in your house is made of all sorts of things—not just skin, wool, hair, dirt, and food from inside your house, but also outdoor things: soil, plants, animal fur, bits of planets, or particles of the Moon. This dust from outer space is called space dust or cosmic dust. Astronomers can detect lots of cosmic dust out in the universe. Our planet travels in a vast cloud of dust specks that orbit the sun. Asteroids—rocky bodies that bump into one another out in space—create some of this dust. When asteroids hit moons, moon dust spreads as well. Dust also comes from comets, which are made of ice and dust and create a dusty trail as they travel through the universe. Some dust is made of stars. When a star goes "supernova," it explodes, sending small particles of dust far out into space.

Every day, this cosmic dust, from many sources, falls on Earth. Some of this dust is swept up in our atmosphere and slowly sifts down toward the ground. Larger pieces of comets hit the atmosphere at high speeds and burn up, creating streaks of light we call shooting stars. The melted, minuscule remains of these shooting stars are dust. This dust floats in our atmosphere, too. Cosmic dust has probably landed on your head without you even knowing it.

Dust not only travels, it lasts. It can stay in the air for hundreds and thousands of years. Inside your house, you may find powder that Cleopatra put on her feet, or dust that a dinosaur stirred up when it rolled. On your shelf could be the very same dust that Martin Luther King, Jr., brushed off his coat.

This evening some of this dust, from today and years past, will color the sunset we see. Tomorrow, dust from all that has come before will make a sunrise to start your day. And because dust is constantly being created and mixed, no two sunsets—or sunrises—will ever be the same.

For Donnie and
Andrea Rogers,
friends who have
blessed our lives
—A. P. S.

For Jack and Gus
—A. J.

Many thanks to my writers' group:
Lola Schaefer, Mary Quigley, Claire
Ewart, Helen Frost, and Barb Morrow.
It's finally here! Also, my thanks to
dust researcher Dr. Armin Clobes.
—A. P. S.

Stars Beneath Your Bed: The Surprising Story of Dust
Text copyright © 2005 by April Pulley Sayre
Illustrations copyright © 2005 by Ann Jonas
All rights reserved. Manufactured in China.
www.harperchildrens.com

The text type is Swis721 Bold.
Watercolors were used to prepare the
full-color illustrations.

Library of Congress Cataloging-in-Publication Data

Sayre, April Pulley.
Stars beneath your bed / by April Pulley Sayre;
Illustrated by Ann Jonas.
    p.   cm.
"Greenwillow Books."
ISBN 0-06-057188-8 (trade). ISBN 0-06-057189-6 (lib. bdg.)
1. Dust—Juvenile literature. I. Jonas, Ann, ill. II. Title.
QC882.S29 2005 551.51'13—dc22 2004002108

First Edition 10 9 8 7 6 5 4 3 2 1

Greenwillow Books